MAKING A FILM

DEBORAH FOX

EVANS BROTHERS LIMITED

Published by Evans Brothers Limited
2a Portman Mansions
Chiltern Street
London
W1M 1LE

© 1998 Evans Brothers Limited

First published in 1998

All rights reserved. No part of this publication may be reproduced, stored in a retrieval system or transmitted in any form or by any means, electronic, mechanical, photocopying, recording or otherwise, without prior permission of Evans Brothers Limited.

Commissioned by: Su Swallow
Design: Neil Sayer
Photography: Peter Bolton
Illustrator: Liam Bonney/The Art Market

British Library Cataloguing in Publication Data

Fox, Deborah
  People at work making a film
  1.Motion pictures - Production and direction - Juvenile literature
  I.Title II.Making a film
  791.4'3'02

ISBN 0237518279

Printed in Hong Kong by Wing King Tong

Acknowledgements

The author and publisher wish to thank the following for their help:
Peter Mares of Carlton Television; Chris Burt and Jack Gold; Nick Robinson and the cast and crew of *Goodnight Mr Tom* filmed by Carlton Television.
The photograph on page 9 is reproduced with the kind permission of Carlton Television.

Front cover (top right): this is a tracking vehicle. The camera can be mounted on the front or back of the vehicle.

Contents

Getting the go-ahead	8
The film crew	10
Preparing the sets	12
Costume and make-up	14
The camera crew	16
Rehearsals	18
Action . . .	20
. . . and cut	22
The final scenes	24
Post-production	26
Glossary	28
Index	29

Getting the go-ahead

I'm Nick and I have got a part in a film called *Goodnight Mr Tom*. I play a young boy, Willie, who has to be evacuated from London during the Second World War. Willie is sent to the country to live with an old man called Tom. I was really excited when I got this part because it is such an exciting and emotional role.

Coming up with the idea

The idea for this film came from the executive producers, who decide what type of films they want to make.

Because the film will be shown on television, the executive producers have to make sure the television company is happy with the idea and is prepared to give the money to make the film. The executive producers find a

▸ *The director discusses a scene with John (on the left), who plays Tom, and me.*

producer for the film, who must get the film made on time and within the budget. This film is based on a book. The producer hires a scriptwriter who turns the story into a film script.

The script

The producer chooses a director to make the film. When the director read the script, he felt that it needed a few changes. While the scriptwriter and script editor made changes, the producer and director found locations for the film, hired the film crew and cast the parts.

Casting

The casting director makes a shortlist of actors for the different roles. I met the casting director last year when she saw me in a theatre production. She thought I would be ideal for this part and she talked to the producer and director. When I met the director, we talked about the role and I read out a few scenes for him. Both he and the producer agreed that I should get the part.

Film language

film crew: the team of people making the film.
film set: the artificial setting created by scenery and other props.
take: the scene shot on film after rehearsals. Usually two or three takes are shot, sometimes more.

I'm eleven and I started singing, dancing and acting when I was seven. Someone told me about a drama group I could go to every Thursday. I need to have a special licence giving me permission to act in films and theatre productions because I am still at school.

The film crew

The director is involved in the script, in casting, in finding locations and hiring a film crew. He has to look at the film script and decide how to film each scene. There are over 200 scenes in this script. We are filming for six weeks in different parts of the country and it is the director's job to keep to the film schedule. If he overruns, then the film will go over budget.

Finding the locations

The location manager had about four weeks to find different locations for the film. The house where Tom lives is next door to a churchyard in a small village.

▲ The village location. Bad weather can cause delays in the filming schedule. The cameras have to be protected from the rain.

◀ The electricians set up the power supply for all the lights before filming in the railway station, one of the locations in this film.

The production designer and the location manager found three villages that were suitable. The producer and director visited the villages and made the final choice.

Assistant directors

Because the director has such a big job to do, he has an assistant to help him. The first assistant director helps the director organise the filming. The first assistant director and the associate producer create a film schedule, which is a breakdown of all the scenes in the film and the days on which they will be filmed. The director has to approve the schedule. The first assistant director also has to organise the film set for the director. He must make sure that everything needed for the scene is there on time so that the director can concentrate on shooting the scene. The first assistant director has two assistants. The second assistant director helps him organise all the paperwork and the hiring of extras, and the third assistant director organises the actors and the props on the film set.

> The cottages in this village are very idyllic, but we have to think about what they would have looked like in 1940. We can't show any TV aerials or anything that looks too modern. We have hired the cottage from the owners. They have moved away during filming.
>
> Russell, location manager

◀ The director, on the right, discusses with his first assistant director, where he would like the camera for the next scene.

Preparing the sets

It is the production designer's job to recreate the world the writer has portrayed, which can take weeks of planning. The designer thinks about how each scene should look – the inside of Tom's cottage, for example, and a railway station in 1940. The art department and the property department (or 'props') make sure that every scene looks just as the designer has pictured it.

Set dressers place all the objects in the correct position before filming.

Creating an illusion

The art and props departments have hired some props, such as furniture,

▲ The set dressers and construction department build an air-raid shelter in the garden of the cottage. It took them half a day to build this shelter.

◄ The railway station has to look like a station in the 1940s. Parts of the train need to be painted, posters are put up in the station and the clock has to show the correct time for the scene that will be filmed later in the day.

bicycles and a steam train. They also had to get some of the props made, for example the gravestones. The 'new' gravestones are made from plaster and can be easily moved. One needs to look older and so parts of the stone are painted to give the effect of age. The assistant from the art department finds clumps of long grass to make the gravestone look overgrown.

▼ *Tracks have been laid behind the gravestone so that the camera can move smoothly towards it.*

Costume and make-up

There are about 50 actors who have been hired for the scenes at the railway station. They are known as 'extras'. They arrive at 8am, giving them enough time to have their costumes fitted and their make-up done. The costume department has a list of all the extras and their sizes and has ordered costumes for all of them.

> First of all I read the script and I make notes on whether the scenes are in the morning or the afternoon, what all the characters are wearing and whether they change clothes. I have about five weeks to research what people wore at that time and to get all the costumes together. I have to make sure I don't overspend on my budget.
>
> Liz, costume designer

▲ ▼ A room has been set up in a local hotel so that the costume team can get all the extras ready in time.

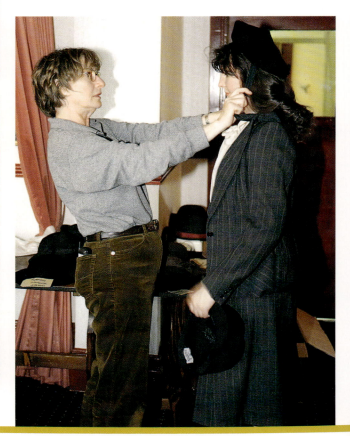

> The first assistant director hires me. We have worked together before. I do all the paperwork and arrange everything the first assistant director needs for filming. If he needs 50 extras for a scene, I will organise that. Every day I let the first assistant director know what I have done.
>
> Steve, second assistant director

Hairstyles and make-up

The make-up team research the hairstyles and make-up for 1940 to make them historically accurate.

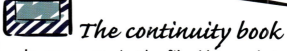

The continuity book

In one scene in the film I have a lot of cuts and bruises. Sally, who does my make-up, had to create these and make them look realistic. The wardrobe and make-up teams always take lots of photographs of all the actors and how they look from scene to scene. If a scene has to be filmed again, then they can look at the photographs and make sure the characters look exactly the same. They keep a book of all the photos and their notes, known as the 'continuity book'.

▼ Pinning the hair is essential before shooting.

The camera crew

▲ The camera crew uses the stand-in actor as a guide while setting up the camera. I practise riding my bike.

▼ I now stand in front of the camera ready for the rehearsals.

Before we rehearse the scenes, the camera crew sets up the camera. This can take quite a long time and so the crew uses 'stand-in' actors.

Director of photography

The director of photography supervises the camera crew and the lighting department. He discusses with the director how the scene should be filmed and lit, and he and his crew must achieve the right results.

The camera is positioned in the best place to capture the action on film. The director may want the camera to film a close-up, where the camera concentrates on the face of one actor; he may want a wide shot where the camera films the action from a distance. If a high shot is needed, the camera can be hoisted on to a crane to film the action from above.

Tracking shots

The crew can't simply push the camera along the ground or along the railway

◁ The director of photography looks through the camera lens to make sure he is happy with the set-up of the shot.

> The art department creates the sets and our job is to make the most of the wonderful sets. The interesting thing about this shoot is that we have been working in tiny locations. It has been tricky trying to get all the people we need into the tiny rooms. It's nice to have a railway platform to work from because it gives us much more space.
>
> Chris, director of photography

platform. The camera would feel every lump and bump! A special track has to be built so that the camera can move along it smoothly. The camera can also be secured to the front or back of a tracking vehicle, which can be driven at speeds of up to 90 kilometres per hour!

Behind the lens

Camera operator: looks through the lens and films the action.
Camera grip: guides the camera and gets it into position.
Focus puller: focuses the camera lens.
Clapper/loader: operates the clapperboard and loads the film into the camera.
Video assistant: sets up the director's monitor and makes a list of all the camera takes.

▲ The camera grip will gently roll the camera along the track. Sometimes the crew uses a special spray on the wheels to stop them squeaking. The track is kept in place by the wooden wedges.

Rehearsals

"Standby for rehearsal," shouts the first assistant director, which means I need to get into position. The director watches closely as I say my lines. He often makes suggestions to me on where I stand or how I say my lines. He is really helpful. Because I have to speak with a London accent, the dialogue coach helps me with rhythm and pronunciation. He listens to the dialogue through his headphones.

▲▶ The director gives me advice on my lines and discusses the scene with me and the actress who plays my mother. Standby props have given us 'gas-mask boxes'.

◀ One of the props team sprays smoke under the train.

Creating effects

In the scenes at the railway station, the director wants a shot of smoke from the steam train as it rolls into the station. The props team can create the smoke by using a smoke-generator device.

The props team

As well as hiring all the props for the sets, the props department organises the personal props for all the actors,

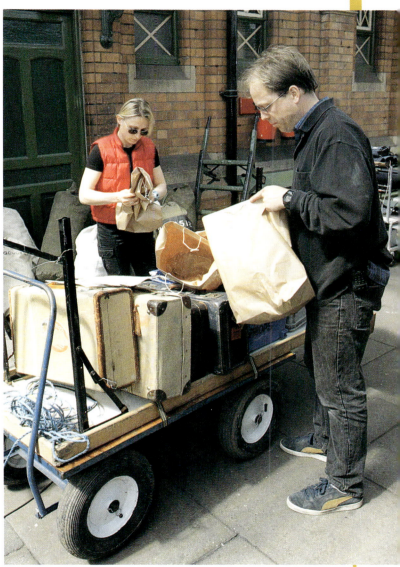

▲ An assistant and a set dresser sort out the pile of suitcases that will be in the background of one of the scenes.

for example bags, guns, gas-mask boxes, cigarettes and suitcases. This is the responsibility of 'standby props'.

Action ...

After two or three rehearsals the director says that we are ready to shoot the film. Everyone has to be extremely quiet on the set because the sound recordist can pick up a cough or a whisper. When we film at the village, the location crew have to stop cars coming near the set because the microphone will pick up the sound of the engines.

"Turnover," shouts the first assistant director, which means that the camera operator has to turn the camera over, or get it started. This takes a few seconds. Then the sound recordist shouts "Speed", which tells everyone that his sound recording equipment is running at the correct

▲ The sound recordist and the director. The director is watching what the camera is filming on his monitor.

▶ The clapperboard is a method of recording which scene the crew is filming and which take it is.

speed. Then the director tells the actors that filming has started when he shouts out "Action".

Watching the action

The director can view everything the camera films on his monitor, or screen. It is the job of one of the camera crew to set up the monitor. The director, sound recordist and dialogue coach listen to the dialogue and background sound through their headphones.

I record the actors speaking their lines as the camera crew films the scene. The boom operator holds the boom microphone above the actors as they speak. Sometimes background noise can be a problem. Small 'planes from local flying clubs fly over the film set regularly. Usually we aim to record 90% of the sound as we film. But if there is unwelcome background noise, then I record a sound 'guide' and the dialogue has to be recorded again in post-production.

Bruce, sound recordist

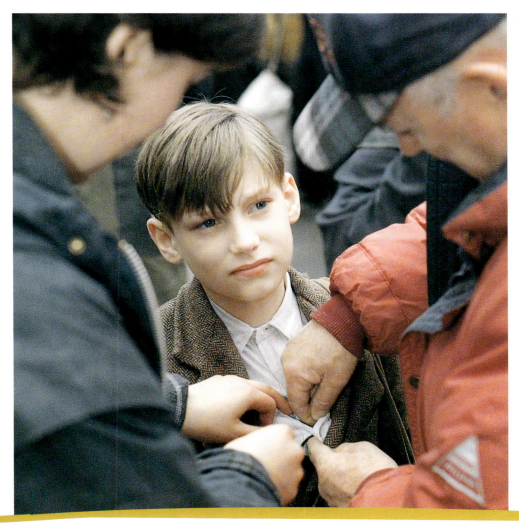

◄ The sound crew attach a microphone to my clothes because I don't speak as loudly as the other actors in these scenes. The radio microphone picks up what I am saying more clearly.

... and cut

After three takes the director is happy with the results. It's time for lunch. The caterers are cooking for over 140 people today, but luckily I am allowed to go to the front of the queue! I have my own room in one of the location caravans. After lunch, I have to spend some time on schoolwork.

◀ Janet, my tutor and chaperone, teaches me for three hours every day.

◀ The lighting team set up a 6000-watt light outside the cottage window to create extra background light.

▲ These rolls of coloured plastic are known as 'gels'. The plastic is sticky-taped over the face of the light to change the effect. Orange gives a much warmer light, and blue gives the impression of daylight.

Setting up the lights

Each scene must be bright enough for the camera to see the actors. Most of the outdoor scenes have been filmed in daylight, but there are some scenes at night and lights have to be used to create the right atmosphere. Natural light is too weak for the indoor scenes, and so extra lights are needed to create a cosy setting, or to illuminate the actors' faces or particular parts of the set.

The lighting team

Sparks: the nickname for the lighting team.
Gaffer: the person in charge of the electricians. The director of photography tells the gaffer which lights to set up.
Best boy: the gaffer's assistant.
Genny operator: the person who looks after the generator that provides electricity for the lighting.

◀ The camera crew needs extra background light because it is filming inside the train. The huge white board reflects light into the carriage.

23

The final scenes

The make-up artist needs to give me a 'cut' knee for the scene where I ride my bike down the hill. My hair is shorter in this part of the story and so the hairdresser has just cut it.

Script supervisor

If I forget any lines during rehearsals, the script supervisor will prompt me. She also makes notes on her script about what we are wearing and what

> It's a really interesting job because I am involved right at the start. I read through the script when it comes in to make sure that it is the right length. If it is too long, the scriptwriter will need to cut it. I have to be really observant and write lots and lots of notes.
>
> Pauline, script supervisor

▲ Using colouring and a sponge, the make-up artist creates my cut knee.

▶ When the takes have been filmed, the script supervisor makes notes on the length of the scene, the size of the camera lens and whether the director preferred one of the takes.

props we all have. The costume department takes photographs of us too. It is the script supervisor's job to keep notes on continuity, on any dialogue problems and the director's preferences.

Rushes

At the end of each day, the film that the camera crew have shot is delivered to the editor. The pictures and sound are matched up, so that everyone can view the pictures and sound together. This film is known as the 'rushes'. The editor sends a video copy to the director and producer, which they can watch that day. If they are unhappy with any part of the film, then it can be shot again. If they prefer, for example, one of the close-ups, they can let the editor know.

▼ *The chalk marks show where I need to stop after riding my bike down the hill. The wedge under the wheel stops my bike moving forward when they film me talking to Tom. The flaps around the camera lens prevent too much light getting into the lens.*

Post-production

When the filming comes to an end, the post-production work starts. Two days after the end of the shoot, the editor has shaped the huge mass of material into the story. This is known as the 'rough cut'.

> I edit the film on computer. I choose the best pictures to tell the story. I look at the notes from the script supervisor and my own notes on the number of shots and the choice of camera angles I have.
>
> Jamie, editor

▲ When the rushes arrive after a day's filming, the assistant editor lists every shot and every take. The editor can call up on the computer different shots from one scene.

From rough cut to fine cut

The director watches the rough cut and then works with the editor to refine the film. At this stage the film is cut to the required length – 102 minutes. After two and a half weeks of intense work, looking at every scene and shot, the film is ready to show to the producer. This version is known as the 'director's cut'. The producer discusses possible changes to the film with the director and editor. They then make the changes and show the revised version, the 'fine cut', to the executive producer.

 Music

Music is very important in films because it creates different moods and feelings. A composer is hired to work on the music for the beginning and end of the film, and for scenes during the film. When the fine cut has been approved by the executive producer, the composer comes in to the studio to make notes on where in the film music is required and the style of music needed.

▼ The editor uses two computer screens. The screen on his left, shown below, acts as his filing system.

▲ The editor and director discuss one of the scenes and the use of the close-up.

The final stages

As soon as everyone is happy with the music, then musicians record it. The sound editor checks the quality of the film sound. Separate sound effects need to be added, such as the sound of a door slamming or a baby crying. These sounds are recorded and added in.

Then the picture quality of the film is checked by a film laboratory. One of the scenes is supposed to be set at twilight, but the crew couldn't film it at that time of the day. The staff at the film laboratory can change the colour on the film to recreate twilight.

Finally the graphics team designs the lettering for the opening and closing stages of the film – the 'credits'. The director and producer approve these.

> I find the process of putting the film together magical because everything is coming together – the pictures, the sound, the music, everything.
>
> Jack, director

> Two months have passed since the last day of the shoot and the director can now sigh with relief! The film is finished. The publicity team will now take over, getting as much publicity for the film as it can before the film is screened. I will do an interview with the press officer to talk about my role.

Glossary

air-raid shelter a building to keep people safe from attacks by aircraft dropping bombs

associate producer the person who is responsible for the management of the film production; the associate producer reports to the producer

boom a pole supporting an overhead microphone

budget the total amount of money given for a specific project over a set period of time

continuity logical sequence; the scenes in the film must look consistent

credits a list of all the people involved in the production of a film or other television programme

dialogue the lines or conversation spoken by the actors in a film or play

extra an actor hired on a temporary basis, usually for a crowd scene

post-production all the work on the film that happens as soon as the filming has finished

press officer person who is responsible for getting publicity for the film

prop any movable object used on the set of a stage play or film

script the written text of a play or film that will be performed by actors

set the scenery and other props used in the location of a theatrical or film production

stand-in actor someone employed to occupy an actor's place while lights and cameras are prepared

take a scene filmed without stopping the camera; usually a few takes are filmed from which the best will be chosen

tracking shot a scene photographed from a moving camera

tracks rails along which the camera rolls

wardrobe the costume department

Index

actors 9, 11, 14, 15, 18, 19, 21, 28
art department 12, 13, 17
assistant directors 11, 15, 18, 20
assistant editor 26
associate producer 11, 28

best boy 23
boom 21, 28
budget 9, 10, 14, 28

camera 10, 11, 17, 24, 25, 28
camera crew 16-17, 21, 23, 25
camera grip 17
camera operator 17, 20
casting 9, 10
caterers 22
clapperboard 17, 20
composer 26
continuity 15, 25
costume department 14, 25, 28
costume designer 14

dialogue coach 18, 21
director 9, 10, 11, 16, 18, 20, 21, 22, 25, 26, 27
director of photography 16, 17, 23

editor 25, 26
electricians 10, 22
executive producer 8, 26
extras 11, 14, 15, 28

film laboratory 27
focus puller 17

gaffer 23
genny operator 23
graphics 27

hair 15, 24

lighting department 16, 22
lights 10, 22, 23
lines 18, 22, 28
location manager 10, 11
locations 9, 10, 17, 20

make-up 14, 15, 24
microphone 20, 21, 28
money 8, 28
music 26, 27

post-production 21, 26-27, 28
producer 9, 11, 25, 26, 27
production designer 11, 12

property department 12, 19
props 11, 12, 13, 18, 19, 25, 28
publicity 27, 28

rehearsals 16, 18, 20, 24
rushes 25, 26

schedule 10, 11
script 9, 10, 24, 28
script editor 9
script supervisor 24, 25, 26
scriptwriter 9, 24
set 9, 11, 12-13, 28
set dressers 12
sound editor 27
sound effects 27
sound recordist 20, 21
standby props 18, 19
stand-in actors 16, 28

'take' 9, 20, 24, 26, 28
television company 8
tracking shots 16, 28
tracks 13, 17, 28
tutor 22

wardrobe 15, 28